THE PROMISED LAND

✦ the Birth of the Jewish People ✦

NEIL WALDMAN

BOYDS MILLS PRESS

Acknowledgments

Thanks to Rabbi Elliot Stevens for his constructive criticism and sensitive reading of the manuscript. Thanks also to Marc Broxmeyer, Andy Leibman, Myron Zackman, Tom Schaeffer, Paul McGregor, and Paul Bernstein, who posed before my camera as models for the Israelites.

Published by Boyds Mills Press, Inc.
A Highlights Company
815 Church Street
Honesdale, Pennsylvania 18431
Printed in China
Visit our Web site at www.boydsmillspress.com

Publisher Cataloging-in-Publication Data

Waldman, Neil.
The promised land: the birth of the Jewish people / written and illustrated by Neil Waldman. 1st ed.
[32] p. : col. ill. ;   cm.
Summary: The story of the Jewish people from Abraham to Moses.
ISBN 1-56397-332-4
1. Jews—History—Juvenile literature.
2. Bible. O.T.—History of Biblical events—Juvenile literature.
3. Bible. O.T.—Biography—Juvenile literature.
(1. Jews—History. 2. Bible. O.T.—History of Biblical events.
3. Bible. O.T.—Biography.) I. Title.
909/.04/ 924 21   CIP   DS118.W35 2002
2001096394

First edition, 2002
The text of this book is set in 16-point Berkeley Book.

10 9 8 7 6 5 4 3 2 1

To Marc Broxmeyer—
My dear friend
I am ever thankful
that your keen mind
brave heart
and gentle gaze
have illuminated my path

HARAN

MOAB

CONTENTS

~ONE~

There are no Phoenicians in the world today. Neither are there any Philistines, Canaanites, Jebusites, or Babylonians. All were defeated on ancient battlefields and dispersed throughout the empires of their conquerors. Over the centuries, they have all disappeared, vanishing completely from the face of the earth. Even the present-day citizens of Egypt, Greece, and Rome spring from nations and religions that have supplanted the great civilizations that once thrived there.

Among the cultures of the ancient Mediterranean world, only the Jews have persisted. Their religion has remained intact since the days of Baal, Zeus, Cleopatra, and the pyramids. Their earliest laws and writings are still revered by members of their faith throughout the world. Their original teachings and commandments are observed by present-day practitioners from Australia to Zimbabwe.

How has this happened? How have the Jews managed to cling to their ancient ways? And how, against all odds, has this small people refused to die?

An answer to these questions may be found within a tale that has been passed from generation to generation for more than thirty-five hundred years. Found in Genesis, the first book of the ancient

Hebrew scroll known as the Torah, is the story of the Jewish people's origin. This story provides an important key to understanding the epic question of their remarkable and unlikely survival.

In the deserts of a land called Haran, a good and decent nomadic tribesman named Abram was visited by God. And God told Abram, "Journey out from your native land and leave your father's house. For I will bring you into a rich new land.

There, you shall grow into a great nation.
I shall give you my blessing;
and I will make your name known
to all the people of the earth."

Trusting God's words, Abram prepares to leave the land and people he has always known. He journeys out of Haran, searching for the mystical land of Canaan, where God has promised that Abram's children and grandchildren will thrive and prosper.

In the process, a profound connection is forged that will endure for thousands of years. It is the relationship of a wandering desert people to a cherished piece of fertile soil, a land that will come to represent their hopes, dreams, and aspirations. They will refer to it as Canaan, *Eretz Yisrael* (the Land of Israel), the Land Flowing with Milk and Honey—and the Promised Land.

Abram's descendants will be defeated and driven from their homeland again and again throughout the centuries. Their dispersions will come to be known as the Diaspora. During years of

exile, they will endure slavery, bigotry, segregation, and attempted genocide. From distant shores, they will retell their children the mythic stories of their beloved homeland and the God that once led them there. And these stories will rekindle their yearning to return to the land of their ancestors. Somehow, within each Diaspora, they will manage to find a way to return. Their fabled first journey back to the Promised Land is known as the Exodus.

·T W O·

To understand the undercurrents of meaning found within Exodus, we must first return to the scroll of the Torah. In ancient times, the Jewish people ritualized the stories found within the Torah by reading the scroll in its entirety throughout the year. Beginning with the reading of the story of the world's creation during a holiday called *Simchat Torah*, the scroll is divided into segments that are read every week. The readings are completed by year's end with the story of the exodus through Sinai and the arrival of the Israelites at the border of the Promised Land. Then, on each ensuing *Simchat Torah*, the cycle begins once again.

And so through the generations, these stories have become deeply embedded in the collective memory of the Jewish people. Not only do Jews throughout the world reread the stories of the Torah again and again, but they also discuss and debate the meanings hidden within each story. Over the centuries, the great rabbis have written down their interpretations, delving into the many layers of symbolism, attempting to uncover the deeper significance of the words. Their writings have been placed within a series of books known as the Talmud. And the Talmudic interpretations are read each week, along with the Torah.

Throughout the generations, Jewish children have heard these stories in their homes, synagogues, and schools. As the Jews were dispersed throughout the world, wandering from country to country, teachers, rabbis, and parents continued to recite the ancient tales. Boys and girls would listen as their elders recounted the stories of the covenant between God and the Jewish people, explaining that if they were faithful to God's law, God would gather them from the farthest corners of the earth and return them to the land of Israel. During times of pain and suffering, generations of Jews continued to dream of the day when they themselves would step onto the sacred soil of their ancient homeland.

13

Stories of God's promise are found throughout the length and breadth of the Torah, beginning with Abram, the first Jew.

Following God's commands, Abram led his people out of Haran. They passed through the Syrian desert, arriving at last in the land of Canaan. And as Abram walked onto the fertile ground of his new home, God appeared to him again saying, "You shall be called Abram no longer. Your name shall be Abraham, 'Father of the Nation.' And the land on which you now stand shall be yours forever, an everlasting possession for you and your offspring."

THREE

Thus the Jewish people is born. But who were these first Jews? How did they live? And what were they like? Upon deeper consideration of the tale of this tribe, and the location and circumstances just described, it is possible to gain some insight into their nature. We know that they were one of many nomadic tribes who herded their flocks through the arid lands east of Israel. Living in tents, they traveled from oasis to oasis in order to find water for their sheep, goats, and cattle. In all likelihood, they journeyed in circular routes, knowing exactly where precious water might be found each season. These watering places were probably known to the tribes since the dawn of human habitation in the desert wilderness.

But then, under the urgings of their chieftain, the people of one particular tribe pack up their tents and leave their familiar surroundings in search of a distant land they have never seen. It can be surmised that Abraham must have been a strong-willed man, a powerful leader, capable of convincing his followers to trek

with him into the unknown. It also seems probable that those who chose to join Abraham were among the most zealous and loyal members of the tribe.

And so Abraham and his followers journeyed through the desert and settled in Canaan. Then, as days passed into months and years, the good land yielded its bounty to their offspring. They multiplied, prospered, and became a powerful nation. Then God appeared to Abraham's grandson Jacob in a dream saying:

"I am the God of your grandfather Abraham, and the God of your father, Isaac. Behold the ground on which you are sleeping. This I give to your offspring. Your descendants shall be like dust in the wind; you shall go out to the east and the west, the north, and the south. But remember, I am with you. Obey my laws and I will protect you wherever you go. I will gather you up from the nations whither I have cast you, and I will always return you to this land."

Twelve sons are born to Jacob, each growing to become the patriarch of one of the twelve tribes of Israel. And it is during their lifetimes that a terrible famine descends upon Canaan. Crops wither and die, until the people are almost without food. For seven long years, the winter rains fail to arrive. And so the great-grandchildren of Abraham gather their families, load their wagons, and travel to Goshen, in the land of Egypt.

Years later, the Jews are enslaved by the Pharaoh, and their courage, tenacity, and passion for freedom will be severely tested. As their suffering increases beneath the whips of their Egyptian taskmasters, the Pharaoh proclaims that all male children born to the Jews will be thrown into the Nile and drowned.

FOUR

Among the Israelite slaves, a male baby was born in the tribe of Levi. And when the child's mother looked into his eyes, she knew that she would be unable to turn her son over to the Egyptians. She kept him hidden for three months. Then, afraid that he would be discovered and killed, she wrapped the baby in a blanket, placed him in a wicker basket, and set the basket adrift in the waters of the Nile.

The daughter of Pharaoh came down to the river to bathe, and as she entered the waters, she spied the basket lodged among the reeds near the water's edge. She ordered her slave girl to fetch it, and when they unwrapped the blanket, they discovered the baby boy.

It is quite ironic that it is Pharaoh's daughter who rescues the baby Moses from the Nile's waters. For when he grows into manhood, it will be Moses who, in turn, rescues the Israelites from the slavery of the Egyptians. Singled out by God to liberate the children of Israel, Moses will become a strong and willful prophet who, like Abraham, leads his people on a treacherous journey through another wild, forbidding desert, searching once

again for the Promised Land. The epic story of their journey fills four of the Torah's five books. The second book bears the journey's name. It is called the book of Exodus.

Moses was reared amid gold and jewels in the palace of Pharaoh. As a member of the royal house of Egypt, he was a young prince and one of the privileged few. But as he ventured beyond the palace walls, Moses witnessed the suffering of his own people. Filled with guilt and rage, he struck down an Egyptian taskmaster who was beating an Israelite slave. He was then forced to flee across the Nile to the safety and solitude of the wilderness of Midian, where he took refuge with a clan of nomadic tribesmen. Moses married the daughter of the tribal chieftain and became an accepted member of the clan.

Moses was alone in the wilderness, herding a flock of sheep, when he spied a spiral of smoke in the distance. He approached and came upon a burning bush. And as Moses looked into the flames, he was astonished to discover that although the fire continued to burn, the leaves and branches of the bush remained as they were. Suddenly, a voice called out from within the bush, and Moses dropped to his knees, bowing before it.

The haunting words that emanate from the bush echo an ancient promise that has been made repeatedly to the people of Israel. Stated yet again in phrases that appear thoughout the Torah, God's voice reverberates with the ancient covenant:

"I am the God of your father, the God of Abraham, the God of Isaac, and the God of Jacob. I have heard the cry of my people in Egypt. I have chosen you to rescue them from their oppressors, and return them to Canaan, a good and spacious land, a land flowing with milk and honey."

As Moses listens to these words, he begins to tremble. He wonders why God has singled him out to attempt such a frightening and monumental task. When doubt creeps into his mind, God teaches Moses to perform several feats in order to demonstrate God's supernatural powers. First, Moses learns how

to transform his rod into a serpent. He then learns how to turn his own smooth skin into the scaly skin of a snake, and finally he learns how to turn water into blood. God then orders Moses to return to Egypt and perform these acts before Pharaoh.

Still, Moses was terribly afraid.

"Please, God," he begged, "I have never been good with words. My speech is halting and my tongue is slow. Please, God, make someone else your agent."

God answered quickly.

"Your brother Aaron the Levite will help you. He speaks quite easily, and now he is setting out to join you. You shall talk with him and put your words onto his tongue. I will always be with the two of you as you speak and tell you what to say."

·◦►FIVE◄◦·

Within a short time, Aaron arrives in Midian. He enters the tent of Moses, and together they return to Egypt to seek out the Pharaoh. And when they finally stand before Pharaoh's throne, Moses utters the legendary words, "Let my people go!" Pharaoh refuses, and so Aaron casts down his rod, and it becomes a snake. But Pharaoh's magicians duplicate the feat, and Pharaoh is not swayed by God's power.

A series of increasingly frightening supernatural acts follow. These are known as the ten plagues. As God metes out the plagues against Egypt, Pharaoh is gradually shaken from his immutable position. First, Aaron touches the Nile with his rod, and all the rivers' waters turn to blood. Then he lifts the rod over the waters, and millions of frogs swim up from the canals, ponds, and rivers. Next, Egypt is covered by lice, then insects, and then swarms of locusts.

These mysterious occurances are the first tangible signs of God's presence witnessed by the nation of Hebrew slaves. Although they do not yet realize it, their journey toward freedom has already begun. The supernatural quality of the plagues is just the beginning of a wide array of unexplicable events that are woven into the entire Exodus tapestry.

As generations of Jewish children read this tale from behind the ghetto walls of Europe, they will continue to hope and dream that these amazing acts of God are real. Perhaps someday, God will return, free them from their oppressors, and deliver them from the lands of the Diaspora.

Now God said to Moses, "I will bring one more plague upon Egypt, a plague more terrible than all the others. After this, Pharaoh will surely let you go. But first, you must prepare for the journey. So gather the whole assembly of Israel and direct each family to sacrifice a lamb. They shall take some of the lamb's blood and put it on the doorposts of their houses, and none shall go outside until morning. They shall roast the lamb and eat it with bitter herbs and unleavened bread. And they shall eat it hurriedly, for it is a Passover offering of God."

Thus the Passover *Seder*, the feast of unleavened bread, is born. This symbolic meal, commemorating the passage from slavery into freedom, is celebrated today by Jews, and some Christians, around the world. At the center of the Passover table is a Seder plate, filled with objects representing things that Passover commemorates.

Central among these objects is the *Pesach*—the roasted shankbone of a lamb, for which the holiday was originally named. Among the primitive agrarian societies of the Middle East, *Pesach* symbolized the rite of fertility. In its earliest form, this ancient ritual celebrated the coming of spring, centuries before the Israelites arrived in Egypt.

The Passover story begins with the words *Avadim hayinu*— "Once we were slaves." It is the goal of the participants to attempt to recall the pain and horrors of slavery in order to appreciate and cherish the freedoms they now possess. During the ceremony, the ten plagues are recited in order, culminating with the last terrible plague that God levels upon Egypt:

"Just before midnight I will go out among the Egyptians, and every firstborn in Egypt shall die, from the firstborn of Pharaoh to the firstborn of the sorcerer and of the slave girl. The blood on your doorposts shall be a sign to me, and I will pass over your houses in the night and spare you. And there will be loud crying throughout the land of Egypt, the likes of which has never been, nor will ever be heard again. And then Pharaoh will allow the people of Israel to leave Egypt."

26

⇒SIX⇐

The Israelites begin their epic journey, surrounded by an amazing assortment of unearthly phenomena. For God has become a pillar of fire by night and a column of cloud by day. Going before the multitudes, God leads them toward the Promised Land.

When they reach the shores of the Red Sea, the Israelites begin to panic, for the Egyptian chariots are bearing down upon them. But once again, God's supernatural powers rescue the children of Israel from impending doom. Directing Moses to lift his rod out over the sea, God now becomes a mighty gust of wind that splits the waters. And as the Israelites cross the sea on dry land, an angel of God is transformed into a great misty cloud that hides them from the Egyptian chariots and protects them. When the Israelites reach the eastern shore, the mist disappears and the wind of God ceases to blow. Within minutes, the Egyptians perish beneath the tumbling waters.

It is no coincidence that this richly crafted drama has continued to captivate believers and nonbelievers alike for more than thirty-five centuries. For the pace of the story is swift, and the characters are remarkably compelling. The ancient verse is filled with the very stuff that epic adventure tales are made of.

28

＊S E V E N＊

And so God delivered Israel that day from the chariots of the Pharaoh. And when the people of Israel witnessed the wondrous and awesome power of God, they sang a song of thanks, and the women danced a dance of joy. Then all the people lay down and rested, and in the morning they began their eastward journey toward the land of their ancestors.

As the Israelites begin their trek across the desolate wilderness, they are overcome with exhaustion. Unable to make sense of their long circuitous route and aching with thirst and hunger, they begin to question their hasty decision to leave Egypt. As whispers of mutiny against Moses and Aaron pass among them, God provides yet another miracle. This time, it is an amazing substance that falls from the heavens.

In the morning, when the Israelites awoke, their camp was covered in dew. And when the dew lifted, a fine and flaky substance lay upon the ground. When the Israelites saw it, they asked one another, "What is this?" And Moses said to them, "It is the bread that God has given you to eat." So the people of Israel went out and gathered it each morning, and when they ate the bread, it satisfied their hunger. And they called the bread manna.

After three months of wandering in the desert, the Israelites arrive at the foot of Mount Sinai. Here they will witness an extraordinary series of supernatural occurrences.

Moses heard the voice of God calling to him from high on Sinai's peak, and he began his ascent. And as the people saw their leader growing smaller and smaller upon the mountain, thunder and lightning shook the sky above him. A dense cloud descended, and Moses disappeared within it.

Then the entire mountain began to quake. The explosions of thunder and lightning quickened, and the noise was deafening. Then, a colossal pillar of smoke erupted from the mountain, reaching upward into the heavens. The earth trembled beneath their feet, and the Israelites were overcome with fear. But then, as suddenly as it had appeared, the storm lifted.

As the days pass into weeks, there is still no sign of Moses, and the people begin to wonder if he will ever return. Confused and frightened, they approach Aaron, who directs them to sculpt a great statue of a golden calf. And when the statue is completed, the

Israelites bow down before it, believing that this is the god that brought them out from Egypt. Aaron then leads the people in a massive celebration, and there is feasting, dancing, and wild merriment.

Within God's cloud upon the mountain, God bequeathed to Moses a great body of knowledge. Then God inscribed ten commandments on two tablets of stone and gave them to Moses. And after forty days and

forty nights upon the mountain, Moses took the tablets of the law in his arms and carried them down from Mount Sinai.

When he saw the golden calf and the wild celebrations, Moses became enraged. He hurled the tablets down, and they shattered at the foot of the mountain. In his rage, Moses saw that the Israelites were wild with frenzy, and he cried out to them, "You have been guilty of great sin!"

But then, as the great prophet looked upon his people, he felt pity in his heart, and he spoke again. "Still," he said quietly, as if speaking to himself, "I will climb back up, and perhaps I can win God's forgiveness."

And the people of Israel looked into their leader's face, and all but a few repented. And so Moses went back up onto the mountain and returned carrying two stone tablets that he himself had carved. And the commandments of God were upon them.

The Ten Commandments will form the cornerstone of a great amalgam of laws, directives, and prophesies that will eventually become the constitution of a new nation. For when the Israelites finally cross the River Jordan and arrive in the Promised Land, they will be transformed from a loosely knit confederation of wandering desert tribes into a powerful nation state. Instead of tents, they will build houses of stone. They will erect villages, towns, and a great walled capital, which will eventually come to be known as one of the great cities of the world. And the ethical and legal backbone of this new society will be the Torah, the Five Books of Moses.

·EIGHT·

So Moses led the Israelites back into the wilderness of Sinai, and the days passed into months and years. And Moses instructed the people concerning all that God had imparted to him on Mount Sinai. And the Israelites built an ark of acacia wood and gold and placed the tablets of the law within it. And they carried the ark with them as they wandered for forty years in the desert. They faced many fierce warrior tribes that blocked the pathway to the Promised Land. And God went before them and crushed all their enemies.

During these forty years, the mixed multitudes of Israelite slaves struggle through a long and bitter rite of passage, and a new nation is forged. Beneath the burning sun of Sinai, the generation that has known the slavery of Egypt gradually dies, and a new generation is born in freedom. It will be this generation's charge to create a new society.

Moses leads his people out from Sinai, onto the rocky steppes of Moab. And for a second time, God instructs him to ascend a great mountain and leave the Israelites behind, saying, "Come alone, and follow Me up from the steppes of Moab to Mount Nebo, onto the summit of Pisgah."

36

When he reached the summit, Moses looked westward into the wilderness. Far beneath him lay the brown and barren desert. In the distance, beyond the desert, a sparkling blue stream snaked its way through the center of a long and narrow valley. And when Moses gazed upon the stream, his eyes widened with excitement. For he knew that, at last, he had set eyes upon the River Jordan, on the edge of the Promised Land!

Beyond the Jordan, Moses could see a land of gently sloping hills, bubbling brooks, and fertile valleys; of lush forests; and meadows sparkling with grasses of every shade of green. Moses could hear the distant singing of birds and the roar of a lion in the mountains.

Moses smiled deeply, for never had he seen a land so rich and beautiful, truly a land flowing with milk and honey.

And God spoke to Moses saying, "This is the land that I promised to Abraham, to Isaac, and to Jacob. And now I give it to your offspring, to possess forever. I have brought you here, to Pisgah, so that you might gaze upon it with your own eyes and hear its music with your own ears. But you shall not pass over Jordan."

And then Moses, servant of God, lay down and died peacefully in the land of Moab, and God buried him near Beth-Peor, in a secret place that no one would ever know. Moses was one hundred and twenty years old when he died; his vision was clear and his energy unabated.

Never again would there arise in Israel a prophet like Moses, who God selected and spoke with, face to face.

The Torah's final sentences leave the Israelites camped alone and leaderless upon the barren steppes of Moab. They remain there in sadness and confusion for thirty days and nights, mourning the death of their most revered prophet.

God then chooses Joshua, Son of Nun, to succeed Moses as their leader. And three days later, as a pink sun rises in the eastern skies, the Israelites awaken and begin packing their tents. With Joshua at the helm, they leave the desert wilderness forever. They cross the River Jordan and step onto the sacred soil of Canaan. Passing through meadows of waving grasses, inhaling the nectars of hillsides flowing with fruit trees, listening to the songs of mountain streams, the Israelites are instantly spellbound.

וַיּוֹצִיאֵנוּ יְיָ אֱלֹהֵינוּ מִשָּׁם

Thus the memories of Canaan's first fragrant petals are pressed into the prayers of the Jewish people. And as the years pass into

decades and centuries, the taste of milk and honey will be embedded in their deepest dreams, where it has remained for more than thirty-five hundred years.

Hebrew Translations

The top borders of all pages read:
Once we were slaves to Pharaoh in Egypt
and God brought us out from there.
Page 3: *A land flowing with milk and honey*
9: *Genesis*
11: *Exodus*
13 *Once we were slaves to Pharaoh in Egypt,*
and God brought us out from there with a mighty hand.
25: *Once we were slaves.*
29: *Jerusalem*